information the organization or website may provide or
recommendations it might make. Furthermore, the author does
not guarantee the accuracy of the information these resources
provide.

The use of any information provided in this book is solely at your
own risk.

A. Explanation of Neuro-Linguistic Programming (NLP)

Neuro-Linguistic Programming (NLP) is a method for understanding and influencing human behavior. It is based on the principle that our thoughts, beliefs, and perceptions can shape our reality.

The term "Neuro-Linguistic Programming" encapsulates three critical facets:

"Neuro" refers to our neurological processes—how we use our five senses to understand the world around us and process information.

"Linguistic" denotes the language and other non-verbal communication systems we use to code, categorize, and give meaning to our experiences.

"Programming" represents the ways in which we can choose our responses and behaviors to achieve our desired outcomes.

NLP, first developed in the 1970s by Richard Bandler and John Grinder, blends insights from linguistics, psychology, and neuroscience. They theorized that successful people have certain thinking and communication patterns that can be modeled and taught to others. Since then, NLP has been used in a wide range of fields, from business and sales to counseling, coaching, and personal development.

B. Overview of the Book

This book is a comprehensive guide to using NLP techniques to overcome procrastination and increase motivation. It's not merely a theoretical work; rather, it offers practical tools and techniques designed to help you better understand and shift your patterns of thinking, feeling, and behaving.

Here's what we'll cover:

In the first section, we will delve into the psychological aspects of procrastination and motivation. We will understand why we procrastinate and what motivates us.

Next, we'll learn about the basics of NLP, its history, and key principles. We will explore how NLP can provide a fresh perspective on procrastination and motivation.

In the subsequent sections, we will look at how NLP techniques can be applied specifically to address procrastination and enhance motivation. We'll learn how to use these techniques to change our habits and behaviors effectively.

The book will then provide real-life case studies of individuals who have successfully used NLP to overcome procrastination and increase motivation.

After this, you will be guided on how to develop your own NLP plan, apply these techniques in your daily life, and track your progress.

Finally, we will address common challenges and solutions in implementing NLP and provide further resources for your NLP journey.

By the end of this book, you will not only have a solid understanding of NLP but also a set of effective tools and techniques that you can apply immediately to start living a more productive and motivated life. Whether you're a seasoned NLP practitioner or a curious beginner, this book will provide valuable insights and practical actions to help you overcome procrastination and increase motivation.

A. The Psychology of Procrastination

Procrastination, in essence, is the act of delaying or postponing tasks that should be done. While it's often regarded as a singular behavior — typically a sign of laziness or poor time management — recent psychological research paints a more complex picture. Procrastination can be understood as an emotional regulation problem, not just a time management one.

First, procrastination often emerges from negative emotions tied to the task — fear of failure, perfectionism, or perhaps the task is boring or unpleasant. When these emotions arise, people tend to cope by delaying the task, providing short-term relief.

However, this relief is temporary. The task doesn't disappear, and the negative emotions often return, creating a vicious cycle of delay and distress. Further, chronic procrastination can lead to guilt, stress, and diminished well-being. Understanding this emotional aspect of procrastination can lead to more effective strategies to tackle it.

B. The Science of Motivation

Motivation is the driving force that induces us to achieve our goals. It is an inner state that energizes, directs, and sustains our behavior. Psychologists have identified two primary types of motivation: intrinsic and extrinsic.

Intrinsic motivation comes from within the individual. It occurs when we find something genuinely enjoyable or satisfying. For example, reading a captivating book because you enjoy the story or playing a game because it's fun.

On the other hand, extrinsic motivation comes from outside influences or rewards, such as money, grades, or recognition. For example, studying hard to get a good grade is an extrinsic motivator.

Recent studies in neuroscience have explored how our brain responds to motivation. The reward system in our brain releases dopamine, a neurotransmitter associated with feelings of pleasure and satisfaction, when we achieve a goal. This dopamine release makes us want to repeat the behaviors that led to the reward, thereby creating a powerful incentive for future action.

C. Relationship between Procrastination and Motivation

Procrastination and motivation are two sides of the same coin. Often, when motivation is low, procrastination is high, and vice versa.

Here's how they interact:

When a task is associated with negative emotions, it's likely that we will procrastinate, even if we recognize the task's importance. The less motivated we are, the more we procrastinate.

Procrastination can decrease motivation. When we procrastinate, we often feel guilty or anxious, which can further reduce our motivation to begin or complete the task.

Motivation can overcome procrastination. When we are motivated, either intrinsically or extrinsically, we are more likely to overcome the tendency to procrastinate.

Understanding this interplay between procrastination and motivation is the first step towards addressing procrastination and increasing motivation. In the subsequent chapters, we will explore how Neuro-Linguistic Programming (NLP) can help us break this cycle, improve our motivation, and overcome procrastination.

A. History and Philosophy of NLP

Neuro-Linguistic Programming (NLP) originated in the early 1970s by co-founders Richard Bandler, a computer scientist, and John Grinder, a linguist. Intrigued by the question of what made certain therapists more successful than others, they began observing and modeling three of the most effective therapists of their time: Fritz Perls, the founder of Gestalt therapy; Virginia Satir, the founder of Family Systems Therapy; and Milton Erickson, a world-renowned hypnotherapist.

From this study, Bandler and Grinder identified patterns of language, behavior, and thought that these therapists consistently used. The co-founders then developed a way to teach these patterns to others, and thus, NLP was born.

The underlying philosophy of NLP holds that an individual's thoughts, feelings, and behaviors are interlinked and influenced by their perception of reality - not by reality itself. Changing these perceptions can, therefore, lead to meaningful changes in thoughts, feelings, and behaviors.

B. Principles and Techniques of NLP

NLP is based on several key principles, including:

The Map is Not the Territory: This principle implies that our perceptions of reality are subjective and not reality itself.

The Body and Mind are Part of the Same System: This principle suggests that our thoughts can influence our bodily functions and vice versa.

There is No Failure, Only Feedback: This principle suggests that mistakes are opportunities for learning.

NLP offers a variety of techniques designed to change our thought patterns and behaviors. Some of the core techniques include:

Anchoring: This technique involves associating a physical gesture or sensation with a particular state of mind.

Visualization: This involves creating a mental image of a desired outcome to increase the likelihood of achieving it.

Swish Pattern: This technique involves replacing a negative thought or behavior with a positive one.

C. Relevance of NLP to Procrastination and Motivation

Given that NLP is primarily concerned with understanding and altering our perceptions and behaviors, it offers a valuable framework for addressing procrastination and increasing motivation.

For instance, using the principle that 'the map is not the territory,' we can understand that our belief about a task (e.g., that it's too hard or boring) may be causing procrastination, rather than the task itself. By changing this belief or perception, we can reduce procrastination.

Similarly, the techniques of NLP, such as visualization and anchoring, can be used to enhance motivation. For example, visualizing the successful completion of a task can increase our motivation to perform that task.

In the following chapters, we will delve deeper into how NLP can specifically help overcome procrastination and boost motivation.

Chapter IV: Neuro-Linguistic Programming and Procrastination

A. Procrastination through the Lens of NLP

Neuro-Linguistic Programming (NLP) offers a unique perspective on procrastination. It does not consider procrastination as a personal flaw or lack of willpower but as a misalignment in our internal programming.

Imagine you're assigned a task. Let's say it's writing a report for work. The thought of this task brings up feelings of dread, boredom, or fear of failure. These negative emotions are signals from your subconscious mind that your perception of this task is unpleasant.

According to NLP, it is this perception, not the task itself, that leads to procrastination. NLP suggests that by changing these perceptions, we can reduce the tendency to procrastinate.

B. NLP Techniques for Understanding Procrastination

NLP offers several techniques to understand and address the root causes of procrastination. One such technique is known as the 'Meta-Model'.

The Meta-Model is a set of questions designed to challenge and expand on the limitations of our beliefs or perceptions. For example, if you believe that writing the report is going to be an arduous process, you could ask yourself:

"What specifically makes me believe that it's going to be difficult?"
"Have I ever done something similar that was not as difficult as I anticipated?"
"What could be a positive outcome of completing this task?"

By challenging these beliefs, the Meta-Model helps uncover the specific thoughts, feelings, and assumptions leading to procrastination.

C. Applying NLP to Overcome Procrastination

Once we've identified and understood the limiting beliefs causing procrastination, we can use NLP techniques to change these beliefs. Here are two common techniques:

Reframing: This involves changing the way you perceive a task to make it more appealing. For instance, instead of thinking, "Writing this report is going to be tedious," you might reframe it as, "Writing this report will hone my analytical and writing skills, and finishing it will give me a great sense of accomplishment."

Anchoring: This technique involves creating a 'positive state' and associating it with a physical gesture or cue. For example, recall a time when you were highly motivated and productive. As you relive that state, make a specific gesture, like tapping your fingers together. With repetition, this gesture becomes an 'anchor' that you can use to instantly evoke the positive state whenever you feel like procrastinating.

Through the lens of NLP, procrastination becomes a habit that can be understood and changed. In the next chapter, we'll look at how we can apply similar principles and techniques to boost motivation.

A. Motivation through the Lens of NLP

Just as NLP offers insights into procrastination, it also provides a valuable perspective on motivation. According to NLP, motivation is not a static trait but a dynamic state that can be influenced by our perceptions, beliefs, and linguistic patterns.

For example, let's say you want to start exercising regularly, but you're struggling to find the motivation. You might think, "Exercise is hard, and I'm not a fit person." NLP suggests that it's these beliefs and the language you use with yourself that are dampening your motivation.

B. NLP Techniques for Boosting Motivation

NLP offers several techniques to enhance motivation. Here are a few of them:

Future Pacing: This technique involves visualizing yourself achieving a goal or completing a task. The goal here is to make the future scenario as vivid and detailed as possible. For instance, if you want to motivate yourself to exercise, visualize yourself running, feeling the sweat on your brow, the rhythm of your breathing, and the sensation of your muscles working. Then, imagine the satisfaction and accomplishment you'll feel when you finish your run.

Swish Pattern: This technique is about creating a strong association between the current state (lack of motivation) and the desired state (feeling motivated). For instance, if the sight of your running shoes makes you feel lazy, you would work with this technique to associate the sight of your running shoes with feelings of energy, strength, and accomplishment.

Positive Anchoring: Similar to how we used anchoring to overcome procrastination, you can create an anchor to trigger motivation. Recall a time when you were incredibly motivated and pair that feeling with a physical gesture. This anchor can then be used anytime you need a motivation boost.

C. Applying NLP to Enhance Motivation

Let's return to the exercise example. You've identified that the belief "Exercise is hard, and I'm not a fit person" is hurting your motivation.

Using the techniques outlined above, you might proceed as follows:

Reframing: Change your belief to something more positive, like "Every step I take towards exercise makes me fitter, and every effort I make is an achievement."

Future Pacing: Visualize yourself exercising regularly, becoming fitter, and feeling the benefits of regular exercise.

Swish Pattern: Associate the sight of your running shoes with the positive feeling of being active and healthy.

Positive Anchoring: Think about a time when you were highly motivated, then create a physical gesture to anchor that state.

By using these techniques, you can shift your mindset and effectively boost your motivation to achieve your goals.

A. Understanding Habit Formation and Habit Loops

Habits, whether they are helpful or harmful, play a vital role in our lives. They're formed through a process called the habit loop, which consists of three elements: a cue, a routine, and a reward. The cue triggers the routine, and the routine, once completed, results in a reward.

For instance, let's say you have a habit of drinking coffee in the morning. The cue might be waking up or sitting down at your desk. The routine is making and drinking the coffee, and the reward could be the caffeine hit or the feeling of a morning ritual.

Understanding this loop is the first step towards changing our habits.

B. Using NLP to Form Productive Habits

NLP techniques can help create productive habits by linking a positive state to the habit we want to form. This process can be done using visualization, anchoring, or reframing.

Let's consider you want to form a habit of meditating daily:

Visualization: Imagine yourself meditating every day. Make the visualization as vivid as possible - feel the calmness, see the setting, hear the ambient sounds, and so on.

Anchoring: Recall a time when you felt peaceful and focused, akin to the state achieved through meditation. Create a physical gesture (like touching your thumb and index finger together) to anchor this state. Use this anchor before starting each meditation session.

Reframing: Change any negative perceptions about meditation (e.g., "It's boring," or "I can't sit still that long") to positive statements, like "Meditation brings me calm and clarity" or "Each moment spent in meditation makes me more patient and focused."

By implementing these techniques, you increase the likelihood of forming the new habit.

C. Using NLP to Break Unproductive Habits

Breaking unproductive habits involves understanding the habit loop and using NLP techniques to change the routine or alter the reward.

Suppose you have a habit of eating junk food when you're stressed. Here's how you might use NLP to break this habit:

Identify the Cue: Recognize the trigger that leads to this habit. In this case, it's stress.

Change the Routine: Use the Swish Pattern to link the cue (stress) with a new, healthier routine (e.g., taking a walk, practicing deep breathing, or drinking a glass of water).

Alter the Reward: Use visualization to imagine the benefits of the new routine (e.g., feeling healthier, losing weight, having more energy). This new reward should be more appealing than the temporary satisfaction of eating junk food.

By applying NLP techniques to the habit loop, we can replace unproductive habits with more beneficial ones.

A. Hypothetical Examples of Overcoming Procrastination with NLP

Case Study 1: John the Writer

John is a novelist who's struggling to finish his latest book. He keeps postponing the task of writing every day. Applying NLP, John realizes that his procrastination stems from his fear of not living up to the success of his previous book.

John uses the Meta-Model to challenge his beliefs: "What specifically makes me believe that this book won't be as good as the previous one?" He identifies his fear of negative criticism and the high expectations he's set for himself.

Using NLP reframing, he changes his belief to: "Every book is different, and each one is an opportunity to explore a new dimension of my creativity." John also uses positive anchoring to evoke his previous experiences of writing joyfully and productively.

Slowly, John starts to feel less intimidated by his project and begins to write consistently.

B. Hypothetical Examples of Enhancing Motivation with NLP

Case Study 2: Lisa the Aspiring Runner

Lisa aspires to run a marathon but struggles to motivate herself to train regularly. Through NLP, she recognizes that she perceives running as a difficult and exhausting task.

Lisa decides to use the Swish Pattern to associate the sight of her running shoes with the feeling of achievement she gets after a run. She also practices future pacing by visualizing herself crossing the finish line of the marathon, focusing on the details - the cheering crowd, the exhilaration, the sense of accomplishment.

Additionally, Lisa uses positive anchoring to recall a time when she felt incredibly motivated and energetic. She associates this state with a specific physical gesture - clenching her fist.

Using these techniques, Lisa successfully increases her motivation. She starts to look forward to her training sessions and slowly progresses towards her goal of running a marathon.

These hypothetical case studies illustrate how NLP techniques can effectively overcome procrastination and enhance motivation. In the next chapters, we'll explore how you can practice these techniques and incorporate them into your daily life.

A. Step-By-Step Guide to Creating an NLP Plan

Identify the Issue: Start by identifying a specific area where you're struggling, whether it's procrastination, lack of motivation, or an unproductive habit.

Understand Your Current State: Identify the beliefs and perceptions that are contributing to this issue. For example, if you're struggling with exercise motivation, you might believe that exercise is too hard or that you're not the athletic type.

Determine Your Desired State: What would you like to feel or believe instead? For the exercise example, a desired state might be: "Exercise makes me feel powerful and energetic."

Choose NLP Techniques: Based on your current and desired states, choose the NLP techniques that will be most helpful. Reframing, anchoring, future pacing, and the Swish Pattern are all potentially useful techniques.

Practice Regularly: Like any new skill, regular practice is key to effectiveness. Make it a habit to practice your chosen techniques daily.

B. Applying NLP Techniques in Everyday Life

Let's say you've identified a procrastination issue with cleaning your house. Here's how you might apply NLP in your daily life:

Reframe: Change your perception of cleaning from "It's a boring chore" to "It's a way to create a more pleasant and comfortable living space."

Anchoring: Create a positive anchor. Think of a time when you felt productive and satisfied, then associate this state with a physical gesture. Use this anchor before you start cleaning.

Swish Pattern: Associate the sight of cleaning supplies with the satisfaction of a clean house.

Future Pacing: Visualize yourself cleaning regularly and enjoying the rewards of a tidy living environment.

C. Monitoring Progress and Adjusting Your NLP Plan

As you implement your NLP plan, it's important to monitor your progress and adjust as necessary.

Journaling: Keep a record of your experiences. This can help you identify patterns, track progress, and make necessary adjustments.

Review: Periodically review your NLP plan. If a technique isn't working as you'd like, don't be afraid to try something different.

Celebrate Success: Recognize and celebrate your progress, no matter how small. This will reinforce your new beliefs and behaviors.

Creating an NLP plan and applying these techniques in your everyday life can significantly help in overcoming procrastination, boosting motivation, and changing unproductive habits. Remember, the key to NLP is consistent practice and flexibility.

A. Common Misconceptions and Pitfalls

Neuro-Linguistic Programming offers powerful tools for self-improvement, but it's important to approach it with a realistic understanding. Here are some common misconceptions and pitfalls to avoid:

Instant Results: One misconception is that NLP offers instant results. While NLP techniques can indeed lead to swift shifts in perception, true change often takes time and consistent practice.

One-Size-Fits-All: NLP is highly individualized, and what works well for one person may not work as effectively for another. Assuming there's a one-size-fits-all solution can lead to disappointment.

Ignoring Underlying Issues: NLP is a powerful tool for changing perceptions and behaviors, but it's not a substitute for professional help if you're dealing with serious mental health issues.

Lack of Practice: NLP is a practical discipline. Understanding the principles intellectually without applying them in your life is unlikely to yield significant changes.

B. Strategies for Overcoming Challenges in NLP Practice

Be Patient: Remember that lasting change often takes time. Don't be discouraged if you don't see instant results. Be consistent and patient with your practice.

Personalize Your Practice: If a particular technique doesn't resonate with you or isn't producing the desired results, don't be afraid to experiment with other methods. NLP offers a rich array of tools - there's likely one that's a good fit for you.

Seek Support: If you're struggling with implementing NLP techniques, consider seeking guidance from an NLP practitioner or coach. They can provide insights, techniques, and support tailored to your specific situation.

Practice Regularly: Make NLP a part of your daily routine. The more you practice, the more natural it will become, and the more effectively you'll be able to shift your perceptions and behaviors.

By being aware of potential pitfalls and equipping yourself with strategies for overcoming challenges, you'll be better prepared to succeed in your NLP journey. Remember, the goal is not perfection but progress, and every step you take brings you closer to your desired state.

Chapter X: Conclusion

A. Recap of Key Points and Techniques

In this book, we've journeyed through the world of Neuro-Linguistic Programming (NLP) and its powerful applications for overcoming procrastination and enhancing motivation.

We've explored the psychology of procrastination and motivation, understanding their interplay and influence on our daily lives. Through NLP, we've seen how we can reshape our thoughts and emotions, altering our behavior to overcome procrastination, and enhancing our drive towards our goals.

We delved into various NLP techniques like the Meta-Model, reframing, anchoring, visualization, future pacing, and the Swish Pattern. We saw how these techniques can be effectively used to alter our perceptions, break unproductive habits, and form beneficial ones.

Through hypothetical case studies, we exemplified the practical application of these techniques. We also learned how to design a personalized NLP plan and how to apply it in our daily lives, including strategies for dealing with challenges along the way.

B. Encouragement for the Journey Ahead

As we wrap up this book, it's essential to remember that change is a journey. It requires patience, persistence, and self-compassion. There might be moments of struggle, but there will also be moments of victory. Embrace the journey and celebrate each small win along the way.

Remember, the power to change your life lies within you. NLP is a tool that can unlock that power, but it's your commitment and willingness to change that will ultimately transform your life.

As you venture ahead on your journey of overcoming procrastination and increasing motivation, keep these words in mind: "The only limit to our realization of tomorrow will be our doubts of today." - Franklin D. Roosevelt.

Step forward with confidence and courage. You have the tools. You have the power. The only thing left is to begin.

Rex Morton is a renowned author and researcher in the United Kingdom with a passionate interest in the human mind, specifically in Cognitive Behavioural Therapy (CBT) and Neuro-Linguistic Programming (NLP).

Morton has spent a considerable portion of his professional life diving deep into the theories and principles that form the backbone of these two compelling fields. His fascination with NLP led him to complete an extensive certification program, solidifying his understanding of this innovative approach to understanding human behaviour.

Although Morton does not have clinical experience, his intense curiosity and dedication to studying these subjects have made him a respected figure in the field. He has thoroughly researched the integration of NLP techniques into CBT, offering fresh perspectives and insights into how these two methodologies can complement each other to enhance understanding of human cognition and behaviour.

As an author, Morton has successfully communicated his knowledge and passion to a broader audience, making complex psychological theories accessible to professionals and interested laypersons. His writing is characterized by a clear, engaging style and a focus on the practical application of theories, making them relevant to everyday life.

In his personal life, Morton is an ardent lover of the natural world, often spending his free time exploring the British countryside. His passion for landscape photography allows him to capture and share the beauty of these excursions. Despite his accomplishments, Morton is known for his humility and eagerness to continue learning. His work continues to inspire those interested in the intricate workings of the human mind and the exciting possibilities presented by the integration of NLP and CBT.

If you've found the content of this book enlightening and wish to continue your journey of understanding the human mind, I warmly invite you to visit my website at www.rexmorton.com. The website serves as a hub of knowledge where I share my latest findings, thoughts, and insights on the integration of NLP and CBT.

I also encourage you to subscribe to the newsletter available on the website. By subscribing, you'll receive regular updates on a range of topics, from detailed discussions on specific NLP techniques and their application in CBT, to the latest research in the field.

The newsletter is also the first place I'll share news of upcoming releases. Whether it's the announcement of a new book, the launch of an online course, newsletter subscribers will be the first to know. This is a great opportunity to continue learning directly from me, deepening your understanding of NLP and CBT, and enhancing your skills in applying these techniques in your own life or professional practice.

I'm looking forward to sharing this journey with you.

www.ingramcontent.com/pod-product-compliance
Lightning Source LLC
Chambersburg PA
CBHW060904260726
48661CB00008B/3457